Birds teach us something very important: To whatever height you rise, you will finally come down to the ground!

MEHMET MURAT ILDAN

THIS JOURNAL BELONGS TO:

....

....

....

....

PAGE	INDEX

PAGE	INDEX

DATE SEEN .... GPS COORDINATES ....

TIME .... LOCATION ....

....

WIND .... WEATHER ....

FIRST SIGHTING [YES] [NO] BIRD SPOTTED/QUANTITY ....

TYPE OF BIRD ....

....

HOW IT WAS DISCOVERED ....

....

....

FEATURES/DESCRIPTION ....

....

....

BIRD'S ACTION/BEHAVIOR ....

....

....

....

YOUR ACTION/COMMENTS ....

....

....

....

....

VIDEO IMAGES TAKEN (FILE NAME) ....

1

BIRD FOTO/SKETCH

NOTES

DATE SEEN .... GPS COORDINATES ....

TIME .... LOCATION ....

....

WIND .... WEATHER ....

FIRST SIGHTING | YES | | NO | BIRD SPOTTED/QUANTITY ....

TYPE OF BIRD ....

....

HOW IT WAS DISCOVERED ....

....

....

....

FEATURES/DESCRIPTION ....

....

....

....

BIRD'S ACTION/BEHAVIOR ....

....

....

....

....

YOUR ACTION/COMMENTS ....

....

....

....

....

VIDEO IMAGES TAKEN (FILE NAME) ....

3

BIRD FOTO/SKETCH

NOTES

DATE SEEN .... GPS COORDINATES ....

TIME .... LOCATION ....

....

WIND .... WEATHER ....

FIRST SIGHTING [YES]   [NO]   BIRD SPOTTED/QUANTITY.................................

TYPE OF BIRD ....

....

HOW IT WAS DISCOVERED ....

....

....

....

FEATURES/DESCRIPTION ....

....

....

....

BIRD'S ACTION/BEHAVIOR ....

....

....

....

....

YOUR ACTION/COMMENTS ....

....

....

....

....

VIDEO IMAGES TAKEN (FILE NAME) ....

5

BIRD FOTO/SKETCH

NOTES

....
....
....
....
....
....

DATE SEEN .... GPS COORDINATES ....

TIME .... LOCATION ....

....

WIND .... WEATHER ....

FIRST SIGHTING [YES] [NO] BIRD SPOTTED/QUANTITY ....

TYPE OF BIRD ....

HOW IT WAS DISCOVERED ....

....

....

FEATURES/DESCRIPTION ....

....

....

BIRD'S ACTION/BEHAVIOR ....

....

....

....

YOUR ACTION/COMMENTS ....

....

....

....

....

VIDEO IMAGES TAKEN (FILE NAME) ....

7

BIRD FOTO/SKETCH

NOTES

8

DATE SEEN .... GPS COORDINATES ....

TIME .... LOCATION ....

....

WIND .... WEATHER ....

FIRST SIGHTING [YES] [NO] BIRD SPOTTED/QUANTITY............................

TYPE OF BIRD ....

....

HOW IT WAS DISCOVERED ....

....

....

....

FEATURES/DESCRIPTION ....

....

....

....

BIRD'S ACTION/BEHAVIOR ....

....

....

....

....

YOUR ACTION/COMMENTS ....

....

....

....

....

VIDEO IMAGES TAKEN (FILE NAME) ....

9

BIRD FOTO/SKETCH

NOTES

DATE SEEN .... GPS COORDINATES ....

TIME .... LOCATION ....

....

WIND .... WEATHER ....

FIRST SIGHTING [YES]   [NO] BIRD SPOTTED/QUANTITY.......................................

TYPE OF BIRD ....

....

HOW IT WAS DISCOVERED...

....

....

....

FEATURES/DESCRIPTION ....

....

....

....

BIRD'S ACTION/BEHAVIOR ....

....

....

....

....

YOUR ACTION/COMMENTS ....

....

....

....

....

....

VIDEO IMAGES TAKEN (FILE NAME) ....

11

BIRD FOTO/SKETCH

NOTES

DATE SEEN .... GPS COORDINATES ....

TIME .... LOCATION ....

WIND .... WEATHER ....

FIRST SIGHTING ☐ YES ☐ NO BIRD SPOTTED/QUANTITY ....

TYPE OF BIRD ....

HOW IT WAS DISCOVERED ....

....

....

FEATURES/DESCRIPTION ....

....

....

BIRD'S ACTION/BEHAVIOR ....

....

....

....

YOUR ACTION/COMMENTS ....

....

....

....

....

VIDEO IMAGES TAKEN (FILE NAME) ....

13

BIRD FOTO/SKETCH

NOTES

....

....

....

....

....

....

14

DATE SEEN .... GPS COORDINATES ....

TIME .... LOCATION ....

....

WIND .... WEATHER ....

FIRST SIGHTING [YES] [NO] BIRD SPOTTED/QUANTITY ....

TYPE OF BIRD ....

....

HOW IT WAS DISCOVERED ....

....

....

....

FEATURES/DESCRIPTION ....

....

....

....

BIRD'S ACTION/BEHAVIOR ....

....

....

....

....

YOUR ACTION/COMMENTS ....

....

....

....

....

....

VIDEO IMAGES TAKEN (FILE NAME) ....

15

BIRD FOTO/SKETCH

NOTES

DATE SEEN .... GPS COORDINATES ....

TIME .... LOCATION ....

....

WIND .... WEATHER ....

FIRST SIGHTING   YES   NO   BIRD SPOTTED/QUANTITY..

TYPE OF BIRD ....

....

HOW IT WAS DISCOVERED ....

....

....

....

FEATURES/DESCRIPTION ....

....

....

....

BIRD'S ACTION/BEHAVIOR ....

....

....

....

....

YOUR ACTION/COMMENTS ....

....

....

....

....

....

VIDEO IMAGES TAKEN (FILE NAME) ....

17

BIRD FOTO/SKETCH

NOTES

DATE SEEN .... GPS COORDINATES ....

TIME .... LOCATION ....

....

WIND .... WEATHER ....

FIRST SIGHTING [YES] [NO] BIRD SPOTTED/QUANTITY..............................

TYPE OF BIRD ....

....

HOW IT WAS DISCOVERED ....

....

....

....

FEATURES/DESCRIPTION ....

....

....

....

BIRD'S ACTION/BEHAVIOR ....

....

....

....

....

YOUR ACTION/COMMENTS ....

....

....

....

....

....

VIDEO IMAGES TAKEN (FILE NAME) ....

BIRD FOTO/SKETCH

NOTES

DATE SEEN .... GPS COORDINATES ....

TIME .... LOCATION ....

....

WIND .... WEATHER ....

FIRST SIGHTING   YES   NO   BIRD SPOTTED/QUANTITY ....

TYPE OF BIRD ....

....

HOW IT WAS DISCOVERED ....

....

....

....

FEATURES/DESCRIPTION ....

....

....

....

BIRD'S ACTION/BEHAVIOR ....

....

....

....

....

YOUR ACTION/COMMENTS ....

....

....

....

....

....

VIDEO IMAGES TAKEN (FILE NAME) ....

21

BIRD FOTO/SKETCH

NOTES

22

DATE SEEN .... GPS COORDINATES ....

TIME .... LOCATION ....

WIND .... WEATHER ....

FIRST SIGHTING | YES | | NO | BIRD SPOTTED/QUANTITY ....

TYPE OF BIRD ....

HOW IT WAS DISCOVERED ....

....

....

....

FEATURES/DESCRIPTION ....

....

....

....

BIRD'S ACTION/BEHAVIOR ....

....

....

....

....

YOUR ACTION/COMMENTS ....

....

....

....

....

....

VIDEO IMAGES TAKEN (FILE NAME) ....

23

BIRD FOTO/SKETCH

NOTES

24

DATE SEEN .... GPS COORDINATES ....

TIME .... LOCATION ....

....

WIND .... WEATHER ....

FIRST SIGHTING [YES] [NO] BIRD SPOTTED/QUANTITY...

TYPE OF BIRD ....

....

HOW IT WAS DISCOVERED ....

....

....

....

FEATURES/DESCRIPTION ....

....

....

....

BIRD'S ACTION/BEHAVIOR ....

....

....

....

....

YOUR ACTION/COMMENTS ....

....

....

....

....

VIDEO IMAGES TAKEN (FILE NAME) ....

BIRD FOTO/SKETCH

NOTES

DATE SEEN .... GPS COORDINATES ....

TIME .... LOCATION ....

....

WIND .... WEATHER ....

FIRST SIGHTING   [YES]   [NO]   BIRD SPOTTED/QUANTITY ....

TYPE OF BIRD ....

....

HOW IT WAS DISCOVERED ....

....

....

....

FEATURES/DESCRIPTION ....

....

....

....

BIRD'S ACTION/BEHAVIOR ....

....

....

....

....

YOUR ACTION/COMMENTS ....

....

....

....

....

....

VIDEO IMAGES TAKEN (FILE NAME) ....

27

BIRD FOTO/SKETCH

NOTES
....
....
....
....
....

DATE SEEN .... GPS COORDINATES ....

TIME .... LOCATION ....

....

WIND .... WEATHER ....

FIRST SIGHTING [YES] [NO] BIRD SPOTTED/QUANTITY ....

TYPE OF BIRD ....

....

HOW IT WAS DISCOVERED ....

....

....

....

FEATURES/DESCRIPTION ....

....

....

....

BIRD'S ACTION/BEHAVIOR ....

....

....

....

....

YOUR ACTION/COMMENTS ....

....

....

....

....

....

VIDEO IMAGES TAKEN (FILE NAME) ....

BIRD FOTO/SKETCH

NOTES

DATE SEEN .... GPS COORDINATES ....

TIME .... LOCATION ....

....

WIND .... WEATHER ....

FIRST SIGHTING [YES]   [NO]   BIRD SPOTTED/QUANTITY.................................

TYPE OF BIRD ....

....

HOW IT WAS DISCOVERED...

....

....

....

FEATURES/DESCRIPTION ....

....

....

....

BIRD'S ACTION/BEHAVIOR ....

....

....

....

....

YOUR ACTION/COMMENTS ....

....

....

....

....

....

VIDEO IMAGES TAKEN (FILE NAME) ....

BIRD FOTO/SKETCH

NOTES

32

DATE SEEN .... GPS COORDINATES ....

TIME .... LOCATION ....

....

WIND .... WEATHER ....

FIRST SIGHTING [YES]   [NO] BIRD SPOTTED/QUANTITY..

TYPE OF BIRD ....

....

HOW IT WAS DISCOVERED ....

....

....

....

FEATURES/DESCRIPTION ....

....

....

....

BIRD'S ACTION/BEHAVIOR ....

....

....

....

....

YOUR ACTION/COMMENTS ....

....

....

....

....

....

VIDEO IMAGES TAKEN (FILE NAME) ....

33

BIRD FOTO/SKETCH

NOTES

DATE SEEN .... GPS COORDINATES ....

TIME .... LOCATION ....

....

WIND .... WEATHER ....

FIRST SIGHTING [YES] [NO]   BIRD SPOTTED/QUANTITY ....

TYPE OF BIRD ....

....

HOW IT WAS DISCOVERED ....

....

....

....

FEATURES/DESCRIPTION ....

....

....

....

BIRD'S ACTION/BEHAVIOR ....

....

....

....

....

YOUR ACTION/COMMENTS ....

....

....

....

....

....

VIDEO IMAGES TAKEN (FILE NAME) ....

BIRD FOTO/SKETCH

NOTES

36

DATE SEEN .... GPS COORDINATES ....

TIME .... LOCATION ....

....

WIND .... WEATHER ....

FIRST SIGHTING | YES | | NO | BIRD SPOTTED/QUANTITY ....

TYPE OF BIRD ....

HOW IT WAS DISCOVERED ....

....

....

....

FEATURES/DESCRIPTION ....

....

....

....

BIRD'S ACTION/BEHAVIOR ....

....

....

....

....

YOUR ACTION/COMMENTS ....

....

....

....

....

....

VIDEO IMAGES TAKEN (FILE NAME) ....

BIRD FOTO/SKETCH

NOTES

DATE SEEN .... GPS COORDINATES ....

TIME .... LOCATION ....

....

WIND .... WEATHER ....

FIRST SIGHTING [YES]   [NO] BIRD SPOTTED/QUANTITY ....

TYPE OF BIRD ....

....

HOW IT WAS DISCOVERED ....

....

....

....

FEATURES/DESCRIPTION ....

....

....

....

BIRD'S ACTION/BEHAVIOR ....

....

....

....

....

YOUR ACTION/COMMENTS ....

....

....

....

....

VIDEO IMAGES TAKEN (FILE NAME) ....

BIRD FOTO/SKETCH

NOTES

DATE SEEN .... GPS COORDINATES ....

TIME .... LOCATION ....

....

WIND .... WEATHER ....

FIRST SIGHTING [YES] [NO] BIRD SPOTTED/QUANTITY ....

TYPE OF BIRD ....

....

HOW IT WAS DISCOVERED ....

....

....

....

FEATURES/DESCRIPTION ....

....

....

....

BIRD'S ACTION/BEHAVIOR ....

....

....

....

....

YOUR ACTION/COMMENTS ....

....

....

....

....

....

VIDEO IMAGES TAKEN (FILE NAME) ....

BIRD FOTO/SKETCH

NOTES

....
....
....
....
....
....

DATE SEEN .... GPS COORDINATES ....

TIME .... LOCATION ....

....

WIND .... WEATHER ....

FIRST SIGHTING [YES] [NO] BIRD SPOTTED/QUANTITY ....

TYPE OF BIRD ....

....

HOW IT WAS DISCOVERED ....

....

....

....

FEATURES/DESCRIPTION ....

....

....

....

BIRD'S ACTION/BEHAVIOR ....

....

....

....

....

YOUR ACTION/COMMENTS ....

....

....

....

....

....

VIDEO IMAGES TAKEN (FILE NAME) ....

43

BIRD FOTO/SKETCH

NOTES

DATE SEEN .... GPS COORDINATES ....

TIME .... LOCATION ....

....

WIND .... WEATHER ....

FIRST SIGHTING [YES]   [NO] BIRD SPOTTED/QUANTITY ....

TYPE OF BIRD ....

....

HOW IT WAS DISCOVERED ....

....

....

....

FEATURES/DESCRIPTION ....

....

....

....

BIRD'S ACTION/BEHAVIOR ....

....

....

....

....

YOUR ACTION/COMMENTS ....

....

....

....

....

VIDEO IMAGES TAKEN (FILE NAME) ....

45

BIRD FOTO/SKETCH

NOTES

DATE SEEN .... GPS COORDINATES ....

TIME .... LOCATION ....

....

WIND .... WEATHER ....

FIRST SIGHTING [YES] [NO] BIRD SPOTTED/QUANTITY ....

TYPE OF BIRD ....

....

HOW IT WAS DISCOVERED ....

....

....

....

FEATURES/DESCRIPTION ....

....

....

....

BIRD'S ACTION/BEHAVIOR ....

....

....

....

....

YOUR ACTION/COMMENTS ....

....

....

....

....

....

VIDEO IMAGES TAKEN (FILE NAME) ....

BIRD FOTO/SKETCH

NOTES

DATE SEEN .... GPS COORDINATES ....

TIME .... LOCATION ....

....

WIND .... WEATHER ....

FIRST SIGHTING ☐ YES ☐ NO BIRD SPOTTED/QUANTITY ....

TYPE OF BIRD ....

....

HOW IT WAS DISCOVERED ....

....

....

....

FEATURES/DESCRIPTION ....

....

....

....

BIRD'S ACTION/BEHAVIOR ....

....

....

....

....

YOUR ACTION/COMMENTS ....

....

....

....

....

....

VIDEO IMAGES TAKEN (FILE NAME) ....

BIRD FOTO/SKETCH

NOTES
....
....
....
....
....
....

50

DATE SEEN .... GPS COORDINATES ....

TIME .... LOCATION ....

....

WIND .... WEATHER ....

FIRST SIGHTING [YES]   [NO]   BIRD SPOTTED/QUANTITY ....

TYPE OF BIRD ....

....

HOW IT WAS DISCOVERED ....

....

....

....

FEATURES/DESCRIPTION ....

....

....

....

BIRD'S ACTION/BEHAVIOR ....

....

....

....

....

YOUR ACTION/COMMENTS ....

....

....

....

....

VIDEO IMAGES TAKEN (FILE NAME) ....

51

BIRD FOTO/SKETCH

NOTES

DATE SEEN .... GPS COORDINATES ....

TIME .... LOCATION ....

....

WIND .... WEATHER ....

FIRST SIGHTING [YES] [NO] BIRD SPOTTED/QUANTITY ....

TYPE OF BIRD ....

....

HOW IT WAS DISCOVERED ....

....

....

....

FEATURES/DESCRIPTION ....

....

....

....

BIRD'S ACTION/BEHAVIOR ....

....

....

....

....

YOUR ACTION/COMMENTS ....

....

....

....

....

....

VIDEO IMAGES TAKEN (FILE NAME) ....

53

BIRD FOTO/SKETCH

NOTES

....

....

....

....

....

....

DATE SEEN .... GPS COORDINATES ....

TIME .... LOCATION ....

....

WIND .... WEATHER ....

FIRST SIGHTING ☐ YES ☐ NO BIRD SPOTTED/QUANTITY ....

TYPE OF BIRD ....

....

HOW IT WAS DISCOVERED ....

....

....

....

FEATURES/DESCRIPTION ....

....

....

....

BIRD'S ACTION/BEHAVIOR ....

....

....

....

....

YOUR ACTION/COMMENTS ....

....

....

....

....

....

VIDEO IMAGES TAKEN (FILE NAME) ....

BIRD FOTO/SKETCH

NOTES

56

DATE SEEN .... GPS COORDINATES ....

TIME .... LOCATION ....

....

WIND .... WEATHER ....

FIRST SIGHTING [YES]   [NO]   BIRD SPOTTED/QUANTITY ....

TYPE OF BIRD ....

....

HOW IT WAS DISCOVERED ....

....

....

....

FEATURES/DESCRIPTION ....

....

....

....

BIRD'S ACTION/BEHAVIOR ....

....

....

....

....

YOUR ACTION/COMMENTS ....

....

....

....

....

....

VIDEO IMAGES TAKEN (FILE NAME) ....

BIRD FOTO/SKETCH

NOTES

58

DATE SEEN .... GPS COORDINATES ....

TIME .... LOCATION ....

....

WIND .... WEATHER ....

FIRST SIGHTING [YES] [NO] BIRD SPOTTED/QUANTITY.......................................

TYPE OF BIRD ....

....

HOW IT WAS DISCOVERED ....

....

....

....

FEATURES/DESCRIPTION ....

....

....

....

BIRD'S ACTION/BEHAVIOR ....

....

....

....

....

YOUR ACTION/COMMENTS ....

....

....

....

....

....

VIDEO IMAGES TAKEN (FILE NAME) ....

59

BIRD FOTO/SKETCH

NOTES

....

....

....

....

....

....

DATE SEEN .... GPS COORDINATES ....

TIME .... LOCATION ....

....

WIND .... WEATHER ....

FIRST SIGHTING ☐YES ☐NO BIRD SPOTTED/QUANTITY...

TYPE OF BIRD ....

....

HOW IT WAS DISCOVERED ....

....

....

FEATURES/DESCRIPTION ....

....

....

BIRD'S ACTION/BEHAVIOR ....

....

....

....

YOUR ACTION/COMMENTS ....

....

....

....

....

VIDEO IMAGES TAKEN (FILE NAME) ....

BIRD FOTO/SKETCH

NOTES

62

DATE SEEN .... GPS COORDINATES ....

TIME .... LOCATION ....

....

WIND .... WEATHER ....

FIRST SIGHTING [YES]   [NO] BIRD SPOTTED/QUANTITY ....

TYPE OF BIRD ....

....

HOW IT WAS DISCOVERED ....

....

....

....

FEATURES/DESCRIPTION ....

....

....

....

BIRD'S ACTION/BEHAVIOR ....

....

....

....

....

YOUR ACTION/COMMENTS ....

....

....

....

....

....

VIDEO IMAGES TAKEN (FILE NAME) ....

63

BIRD FOTO/SKETCH

NOTES

64

DATE SEEN .... GPS COORDINATES ....

TIME .... LOCATION ....

....

WIND .... WEATHER ....

FIRST SIGHTING | YES | | NO | BIRD SPOTTED/QUANTITY ....

TYPE OF BIRD ....

HOW IT WAS DISCOVERED ....

....

....

FEATURES/DESCRIPTION ....

....

....

BIRD'S ACTION/BEHAVIOR ....

....

....

....

YOUR ACTION/COMMENTS ....

....

....

....

....

VIDEO IMAGES TAKEN (FILE NAME) ....

BIRD FOTO/SKETCH

NOTES

DATE SEEN .... GPS COORDINATES ....

TIME .... LOCATION ....

....

WIND .... WEATHER ....

FIRST SIGHTING ☐ YES ☐ NO BIRD SPOTTED/QUANTITY ....

TYPE OF BIRD ....

....

HOW IT WAS DISCOVERED ....

....

....

....

FEATURES/DESCRIPTION ....

....

....

....

BIRD'S ACTION/BEHAVIOR ....

....

....

....

....

YOUR ACTION/COMMENTS ....

....

....

....

....

....

VIDEO IMAGES TAKEN (FILE NAME) ....

67

BIRD FOTO/SKETCH

NOTES
....
....
....
....
....
....

DATE SEEN .... GPS COORDINATES ....

TIME .... LOCATION ....

....

WIND .... WEATHER ....

FIRST SIGHTING [YES] [NO] BIRD SPOTTED/QUANTITY...

TYPE OF BIRD ....

....

HOW IT WAS DISCOVERED ....

....

....

....

FEATURES/DESCRIPTION ....

....

....

....

BIRD'S ACTION/BEHAVIOR ....

....

....

....

YOUR ACTION/COMMENTS ....

....

....

....

....

VIDEO IMAGES TAKEN (FILE NAME) ....

69

BIRD FOTO/SKETCH

NOTES

DATE SEEN .... GPS COORDINATES ....

TIME .... LOCATION ....

....

WIND .... WEATHER ....

FIRST SIGHTING ☐ YES ☐ NO BIRD SPOTTED/QUANTITY ....

TYPE OF BIRD ....

....

HOW IT WAS DISCOVERED ....

....

....

FEATURES/DESCRIPTION ....

....

....

BIRD'S ACTION/BEHAVIOR ....

....

....

....

YOUR ACTION/COMMENTS ....

....

....

....

....

VIDEO IMAGES TAKEN (FILE NAME) ....

BIRD FOTO/SKETCH

NOTES

72

DATE SEEN .... GPS COORDINATES ....

TIME .... LOCATION ....

....

WIND .... WEATHER ....

FIRST SIGHTING | YES | | NO | BIRD SPOTTED/QUANTITY ....

TYPE OF BIRD ....

HOW IT WAS DISCOVERED ....

....

....

FEATURES/DESCRIPTION ....

....

....

BIRD'S ACTION/BEHAVIOR ....

....

....

....

YOUR ACTION/COMMENTS ....

....

....

....

....

VIDEO IMAGES TAKEN (FILE NAME) ....

73

BIRD FOTO/SKETCH

NOTES

DATE SEEN .... GPS COORDINATES ....

TIME .... LOCATION ....

....

WIND .... WEATHER ....

FIRST SIGHTING [YES]   [NO]   BIRD SPOTTED/QUANTITY ....

TYPE OF BIRD ....

....

HOW IT WAS DISCOVERED ....

....

....

FEATURES/DESCRIPTION ....

....

....

BIRD'S ACTION/BEHAVIOR ....

....

....

....

YOUR ACTION/COMMENTS ....

....

....

....

....

VIDEO IMAGES TAKEN (FILE NAME) ....

75

BIRD FOTO/SKETCH

NOTES

DATE SEEN .... GPS COORDINATES ....

TIME .... LOCATION ....

....

WIND .... WEATHER ....

FIRST SIGHTING [YES] [NO] BIRD SPOTTED/QUANTITY...

TYPE OF BIRD ....

....

HOW IT WAS DISCOVERED ....

....

....

....

FEATURES/DESCRIPTION ....

....

....

....

BIRD'S ACTION/BEHAVIOR ....

....

....

....

....

YOUR ACTION/COMMENTS ....

....

....

....

....

....

VIDEO IMAGES TAKEN (FILE NAME) ....

BIRD FOTO/SKETCH

NOTES

DATE SEEN .... GPS COORDINATES ....

TIME .... LOCATION ....

....

WIND.. WEATHER ....

FIRST SIGHTING | YES | | NO | BIRD SPOTTED/QUANTITY..

TYPE OF BIRD ....

....

HOW IT WAS DISCOVERED...

....

....

....

FEATURES/DESCRIPTION ....

....

....

....

BIRD'S ACTION/BEHAVIOR ....

....

....

....

....

YOUR ACTION/COMMENTS ....

....

....

....

....

VIDEO IMAGES TAKEN (FILE NAME) ....

BIRD FOTO/SKETCH

NOTES

DATE SEEN .... GPS COORDINATES ....

TIME .... LOCATION ....

....

WIND .... WEATHER ....

FIRST SIGHTING [YES] [NO] BIRD SPOTTED/QUANTITY ....

TYPE OF BIRD ....

....

HOW IT WAS DISCOVERED ....

....

....

....

FEATURES/DESCRIPTION ....

....

....

....

BIRD'S ACTION/BEHAVIOR ....

....

....

....

....

YOUR ACTION/COMMENTS ....

....

....

....

....

VIDEO IMAGES TAKEN (FILE NAME) ....

BIRD FOTO/SKETCH

NOTES

DATE SEEN .... GPS COORDINATES ....

TIME .... LOCATION ....

....

WIND .... WEATHER ....

FIRST SIGHTING [YES] [NO] BIRD SPOTTED/QUANTITY ....

TYPE OF BIRD ....

....

HOW IT WAS DISCOVERED ....

....

....

....

FEATURES/DESCRIPTION ....

....

....

....

BIRD'S ACTION/BEHAVIOR ....

....

....

....

....

YOUR ACTION/COMMENTS ....

....

....

....

....

VIDEO IMAGES TAKEN (FILE NAME) ....

83

BIRD FOTO/SKETCH

NOTES

DATE SEEN .... GPS COORDINATES ....

TIME .... LOCATION ....

....

WIND .... WEATHER ....

FIRST SIGHTING [YES] [NO] BIRD SPOTTED/QUANTITY.............................

TYPE OF BIRD ....

HOW IT WAS DISCOVERED...

....

....

....

FEATURES/DESCRIPTION ....

....

....

....

BIRD'S ACTION/BEHAVIOR ....

....

....

....

....

YOUR ACTION/COMMENTS ....

....

....

....

....

VIDEO IMAGES TAKEN (FILE NAME) ....

BIRD FOTO/SKETCH

NOTES

DATE SEEN .... GPS COORDINATES ....

TIME .... LOCATION ....

....

WIND .... WEATHER ....

FIRST SIGHTING | YES | | NO | BIRD SPOTTED/QUANTITY ....

TYPE OF BIRD ....

....

HOW IT WAS DISCOVERED ....

....

....

....

FEATURES/DESCRIPTION ....

....

....

....

BIRD'S ACTION/BEHAVIOR ....

....

....

....

YOUR ACTION/COMMENTS ....

....

....

....

....

VIDEO IMAGES TAKEN (FILE NAME) ....

BIRD FOTO/SKETCH

NOTES

88

DATE SEEN .... GPS COORDINATES ....

TIME .... LOCATION ....

....

WIND .... WEATHER ....

FIRST SIGHTING   [YES]   [NO]   BIRD SPOTTED/QUANTITY............................

TYPE OF BIRD ....

....

HOW IT WAS DISCOVERED ....

....

....

FEATURES/DESCRIPTION ....

....

....

BIRD'S ACTION/BEHAVIOR ....

....

....

....

YOUR ACTION/COMMENTS ....

....

....

....

....

VIDEO IMAGES TAKEN (FILE NAME) ....

89

BIRD FOTO/SKETCH

NOTES

....
....
....
....
....

DATE SEEN .... GPS COORDINATES ....

TIME .... LOCATION ....

....

WIND .... WEATHER ....

FIRST SIGHTING [YES] [NO] BIRD SPOTTED/QUANTITY ....

TYPE OF BIRD ....

HOW IT WAS DISCOVERED ....

....

....

....

FEATURES/DESCRIPTION ....

....

....

....

BIRD'S ACTION/BEHAVIOR ....

....

....

....

....

YOUR ACTION/COMMENTS ....

....

....

....

....

VIDEO IMAGES TAKEN (FILE NAME) ....

BIRD FOTO/SKETCH

NOTES

DATE SEEN .... GPS COORDINATES ....

TIME .... LOCATION ....

WIND .... WEATHER ....

FIRST SIGHTING | YES | | NO | BIRD SPOTTED/QUANTITY............................

TYPE OF BIRD ....

HOW IT WAS DISCOVERED ....

....

....

FEATURES/DESCRIPTION ....

....

....

BIRD'S ACTION/BEHAVIOR ....

....

....

....

YOUR ACTION/COMMENTS ....

....

....

....

....

VIDEO IMAGES TAKEN (FILE NAME) ....

93

BIRD FOTO/SKETCH

NOTES

DATE SEEN .... GPS COORDINATES ....

TIME .... LOCATION ....

....

WIND .... WEATHER ....

FIRST SIGHTING [YES]   [NO]   BIRD SPOTTED/QUANTITY...............................

TYPE OF BIRD ....

....

HOW IT WAS DISCOVERED...

....

....

....

FEATURES/DESCRIPTION ....

....

....

....

BIRD'S ACTION/BEHAVIOR ....

....

....

....

....

YOUR ACTION/COMMENTS ....

....

....

....

....

VIDEO IMAGES TAKEN (FILE NAME) ....

95

BIRD FOTO/SKETCH

NOTES

DATE SEEN .... GPS COORDINATES ....

TIME .... LOCATION ....

....

WIND .... WEATHER ....

FIRST SIGHTING [YES]   [NO]   BIRD SPOTTED/QUANTITY ....

TYPE OF BIRD ....

HOW IT WAS DISCOVERED ....

....

....

FEATURES/DESCRIPTION ....

....

....

BIRD'S ACTION/BEHAVIOR ....

....

....

....

YOUR ACTION/COMMENTS ....

....

....

....

....

VIDEO IMAGES TAKEN (FILE NAME) ....

97

BIRD FOTO/SKETCH

NOTES

DATE SEEN .... GPS COORDINATES ....

TIME .... LOCATION ....

....

WIND .... WEATHER ....

FIRST SIGHTING [YES]   [NO]   BIRD SPOTTED/QUANTITY...

TYPE OF BIRD ....

....

HOW IT WAS DISCOVERED..

....

....

....

FEATURES/DESCRIPTION ....

....

....

....

BIRD'S ACTION/BEHAVIOR ....

....

....

....

....

YOUR ACTION/COMMENTS ....

....

....

....

....

....

VIDEO IMAGES TAKEN (FILE NAME) ....

BIRD FOTO/SKETCH

NOTES

DATE SEEN .... GPS COORDINATES ....

TIME .... LOCATION ....

....

WIND .... WEATHER ....

FIRST SIGHTING ☐ YES ☐ NO BIRD SPOTTED/QUANTITY...

TYPE OF BIRD ....

....

HOW IT WAS DISCOVERED ....

....

....

....

FEATURES/DESCRIPTION ....

....

....

....

BIRD'S ACTION/BEHAVIOR ....

....

....

....

....

YOUR ACTION/COMMENTS ....

....

....

....

....

....

VIDEO IMAGES TAKEN (FILE NAME) ....

BIRD FOTO/SKETCH

NOTES

....

....

....

....

....

DATE SEEN .... GPS COORDINATES ....

TIME .... LOCATION ....

WIND .... WEATHER ....

FIRST SIGHTING [YES] [NO] BIRD SPOTTED/QUANTITY..

TYPE OF BIRD ....

HOW IT WAS DISCOVERED ....
....
....

FEATURES/DESCRIPTION ....
....
....

BIRD'S ACTION/BEHAVIOR ....
....
....
....

YOUR ACTION/COMMENTS ....
....
....
....
....

VIDEO IMAGES TAKEN (FILE NAME) ....

BIRD FOTO/SKETCH

NOTES

DATE SEEN .... GPS COORDINATES ....

TIME .... LOCATION ....

....

WIND .... WEATHER ....

FIRST SIGHTING   YES   NO   BIRD SPOTTED/QUANTITY ....

TYPE OF BIRD ....

....

HOW IT WAS DISCOVERED ....

....

....

....

FEATURES/DESCRIPTION ....

....

....

....

BIRD'S ACTION/BEHAVIOR ....

....

....

....

....

YOUR ACTION/COMMENTS ....

....

....

....

....

VIDEO IMAGES TAKEN (FILE NAME) ....

BIRD FOTO/SKETCH

NOTES

Made in the USA
Columbia, SC
08 July 2019